Nobody's life is a bed of roses. We all have crosses to bear, and we all just do our best. I would never claim to have the worst situation. There are many widows, and many people dying of AIDS, many people killed in Lebanon, people starving all over the planet. So we have to count our lucky stars.

Yoko Ono

AIDS can destroy a family if you let it, but luckily for my sister and me, Mom taught us to keep going. Don't give up, be proud of who you are, and never feel sorry for yourself.

Ryan White

When I first found out I had HIV, I had to find somebody who was living with it, who could help me understand my journey and what I was going to have to deal with day-to-day. I found out that a person named Elizabeth Frazier was living with AIDS at the time, and so I called her up, and she took a meeting with me.

Magic Johnson

Our meaning is to make our little planet Earth a better place to live, to stop wars, disarm nuclear missiles, to stop diseases, AIDS, plague, cancer and to stop pollution.

Uri Geller

The United Nations Children's Fund reports that more than 18 million children worldwide have lost both parents to the ravages of AIDS, starvation, war or natural disasters.

Foster Friess

My son has died of AIDS.

Nelson Mandela

I enjoy being the messenger for God in terms of letting people know about HIV and AIDS.

Magic Johnson

Give a child love, laughter and peace, not AIDS.

Nelson Mandela

Because of the lack of education on AIDS, discrimination, fear, panic, and lies surrounded me.

Ryan White

AIDS is not just God's punishment for homosexuals; it is God's punishment for the society that tolerates homosexuals.

Jerry Falwell

Some say that AIDS came from the monkeys, and I doubt that because we have been living with monkeys from time immemorial, others say it was a curse from God, but I say it cannot be that.

Wangari Maathai

The ideal thing would be to have a 100 percent effective AIDS vaccine. And to have broad usage of that vaccine. That would literally break the epidemic.

Bill Gates

My name is Ryan White. I am sixteen years old. I have hemophilia, and I have AIDS.

Ryan White

You look at the large problems that we face - that would be overpopulation, water shortages, global warming and AIDS, I suppose - all of that needs international cooperation to be solved.

Molly Ivins

I lost relatives to AIDS. A couple of my closest cousins, favorite cousins. I lost friends to AIDS, high school friends who never even made it to their 21st birthdays in the '80s. When it's that close to you, you can't - you know, you can't really deny it, and you can't run from it.

Queen Latifah

When we walk away from global warming, Kyoto, when we are irresponsibly slow in moving toward AIDS in Africa, when we don't advance and live up to our own rhetoric and standards, we set a terrible message of duplicity and hypocrisy.

John F. Kerry

I lost relatives to AIDS, a couple of my closest cousins. I lost friends to AIDS, high-school friends who never even made it to their 21st birthdays in the '80s. When it's that close to you, you can't really deny it, and you can't run from it.

Queen Latifah

I'm a real person, and I'm angry. I'm trying to use this celebrity thing to get people some help. AIDS, poverty, racism - I want to be one of the hands that helps stop all that. I'll put it on my shoulders. I'll charge it to my account.

Jamie Foxx

Those who have come into Formula One without experiencing cars devoid of electronic aids will find it tough. To control 800 horse power relying just on arm muscles and foot sensitivity can turn out to be a dangerous exercise.

Michael Schumacher

Electronic aids, particularly domestic computers, will help the inner migration, the opting out of reality. Reality is no longer going to be the stuff out there, but the stuff inside your head. It's going to be commercial and nasty at the same time.

J. G. Ballard

If we ever hope to rid the world of the political AIDS of our time, terrorism, the rule must be clear: One does not deal with terrorists; one does not bargain with terrorists; one kills terrorists.

Meir Kahane

You can't get AIDS from a hug or a handshake or a meal with a friend.

Magic Johnson

HIV infection and AIDS is growing - but so too is public apathy. We have already lost too many friends and colleagues.

David Geffen

We've taken on the major health problems of the poorest - tuberculosis, maternal mortality, AIDS, malaria - in four countries. We've scored some victories in the sense that we've cured or treated thousands and changed the discourse about what is possible.

Paul Farmer

You know it's very difficult to be an actor, and to have people depending on you to say the right line, at the right time, and to not be able to hear your cues! I can't tell you how many times I would've had to have said What? if I didn't have my hearing aids. So my hearing aids are a life saver, and they allow me to practice my craft.

Leslie Nielsen

That's why I wanted to be part of this AIDS Project Los Angeles party. We help raise funds for those who are having a tough time with some very basic necessities, like shelter, food, and medical care.

Brande Roderick

I came into a strong organization, and I hope I strengthened it more and expanded its capacity to deal with some of the challenges that might not have seemed as great 10 years ago, such as H.I.V., AIDS and children affected by war.

Carol Bellamy

It's really important to me to promote worthy causes. But not in a heavy, obligatory, responsibility way. I really admired that as a kid, learning about the 'Elton John AIDS Foundation.' And I was obsessed with The Indigo Girls. And they are the consummate activist group, always reaching out, especially to Native causes and things like that.

Brandi Carlile

The '50s were terrifying with nuclear bomb stuff but boring in a social way, and then the '60s were happening, and remember, there was no AIDS.

Robert Klein

When I work out, I wear two in-the-ear hearing aids for comfort, and then I wear the behind-the-ears for my day-to-day non-physical activities, when I need maximum hearing and to communicate with people and do interviews!

Lou Ferrigno

AIDS is a global problem and there should be a global solution found by the entire international community. It is really scary to see and imagine our world fall into pieces because we refuse to share and put in the common vestiges of our civilizations.

Sarah Polley

I had seen AIDS patients in India and Africa, and knowing that people were dying even though drugs existed that could help them was shattering for me.

Yusuf Hamied

It's an interesting line that I walk. The AIDS crisis has done a lot for my songs and made them proliferate, and my songs have contributed a lot to that cause as well.

David Friedman

The pandemic of AIDS is a gender-based disease.

Stephen Lewis

Roughly speaking, this hypothesis asks whether drug use causes some of the diseases officially associated with AIDS, such as immunodeficiency and Kaposi's sarcoma.

Serge Lang

Questions have also arisen about AIDS being transmitted to hemophiliacs via blood transfusions.

Serge Lang

The bulk of my learning - if I may call it such - has come within the past three months, after I became a part of the fragile body of patients who make up an AIDS hospice. Here, surrounded by teams of supportive nurses, attentive doctors, and interns, one gently comes upon his own strengths and shortcomings.

Lance Loud

Because I found myself telling the story of his family to people without the visual aids that I was able to employ by filming them eventually. But I very much knew exactly what I was going to do.

Terry Zwigoff

It's important not to lose sight of the fact people of all sorts are still putting themselves at risk. It happens to straight and gay, single and married. I have never been comfortable thinking of AIDS as something that 'other people' get.

Brande Roderick

If Carter had been there when the AIDS crisis came up, it would have been a whole different story. It could have been treated like a legitimate disease.

Jean O'Leary

I think it's very important to support the program in your area, as each part of the country has its own challenges coping with AIDS. It can be very different from state to state and city to city. Wherever you live, there is surely someone who could use your help.

Beth Broderick

When AIDS hit, lots of people banded together to take care of each other and do what the government wasn't doing. When you grow up Jewish, as I have, you learn that everybody hates you, no one's going to help you, and you have to take care of yourself. That's a great maxim to the gay community, and we took it to heart; we took care of our own.

Bruce Vilanch

I love biographies. I read Patti Smith's 'Just Kids.' I'm into that time frame in New York, the '70s and '80s. In art school, I read 'Close to the Knives,' the autobiography of the artist and AIDS activist David Wojnarowicz.

Barry McGee

Popular ideas about AIDS are based on a hypothesis that does not stand up to scientific scrutiny.

Nate Mendel

I would just die if some little girl saw me jump into bed with someone in the movies, and then she did it and got AIDS and died.

T'Keyah Crystal Keymah

I have an AIDS ribbon tattooed on my arm.

Ryan Lewis

I'm particularly proud of my work with the Starkey Hearing Foundation for whom I raised a million dollars in one day on 'Celebrity Apprentice.' They do great work around the world helping deaf children in developing countries get proper attention and free hearing aids.

Marlee Matlin

AIDS itself is subject to incredible stigma.

Bill Gates

I know one man who was impotent who gave AIDS to his wife and the only thing they did was kiss.

Pat Robertson

We need men and women to sit down and talk to each other about sex honestly and openly. That would help us fight Aids so immediately. But our lack of communication is hugely problematic.

Emma Thompson

There have been two popular subjects for poetry in the last few decades: the Vietnam War and AIDS, about both of which almost all of us have felt deeply.

Thom Gunn

But it is true that sometimes an enveloping darkness aids one to clearer vision; as in a panorama building, for example, where the obscurity about the entrance prepares one better for the climax, and gives the scene depicted a more real and vivid appearance.

Pierre Loti

It will kill four times as many Americans as AIDS will over the next decade. I feel that what ever kind of disability God has given me, as an entertainer and as a public figure, it is so I can be a representative for others.

Naomi Judd

Diarrhea, 90 percent of which is caused by food and water contaminated by excrement, kills a child every fifteen seconds. That's more than AIDS, malaria, or measles, combined. Human feces are an impressive weapon of mass destruction.

Rose George

China is certainly an important player in the global economy, and a widespread AIDS epidemic would threaten that growth.

Bill Gates

I don't think President Bush is doing anything at all about Aids. In fact, I'm not sure he even knows how to spell Aids.

Elizabeth Taylor

The AIDS virus is not more powerful than God.

Marianne Williamson

But try if you can to support, whether it's AIDS or the cancer foundation, so that someone else might survive, might prosper, and might actually be cured of this dreaded disease.

Jim Valvano

I was destined to work with dying patients. I had no choice when I encountered my first AIDS patient. I felt called to travel some 250,000 miles each year to hold workshops that helped people cope with the most painful aspects of life, death and the transition between the two.

Elisabeth Kubler-Ross

My work with AIDS patients started right at the beginning of the epidemic, totally unplanned and spontaneous, as all my work had proceeded in the previous two decades, if it were not already my whole life-style! In the early eighties, we knew very little about this peculiar disease.

Elisabeth Kubler-Ross

I'm not really religious but very spiritual. I give money to this company that manufactures hearing aids on a regular basis. More people should really hear me sing. I have a gift from God.

Christina Aguilera

I found out through the Internet that I have AIDS. I learned that I was dead. Where else would I find these things?

Layne Staley

I'm grateful for doing those drugs, because they kept me from getting laid and I would have gotten AIDS.

Steven Tyler

I've been to enough other countries in the world to know what happens when you have socialized single-payer health care. It works. People don't get sick as much. They don't lose their life savings with a catastrophic illness like cancer or AIDS.

Jello Biafra

A lot of people in my world - in the acting world - have either lost friends to Aids or live with HIV because its origin in our culture, in New York for instance, was in the gay community.

Emma Thompson

I believe Aids is the most important issue we face, because how we treat the poor is a reflection of who we are as a people.

Alicia Keys

I have learned more about love, selflessness and human understanding from the people I have met in this great adventure in the world of AIDS than I ever did in the cutthroat, competitive world in which I spent my life.

Anthony Perkins

I do not have bad days. I don't wake up in the morning and think that I'm going to get AIDS. I don't dream bad dreams about it. If I did, I'd be giving in to the negativity.

Magic Johnson

AIDS obliges people to think of sex as having, possibly, the direst consequences: suicide. Or murder.

Susan Sontag

I'm the cofounder of Keep a Child Alive. We provide medicine for families affected by HIV and AIDS in places like Africa and India.

Alicia Keys

AIDS is such a scary thing and it's also the kind of thing that you think won't happen to you. It can happen to you and it's deadly serious.

Ice T

HIV AIDS is a disease with stigma. And we have learned with experience, not just with HIV AIDS but with other diseases, countries for many reasons are sometimes hesitant to admit they have a problem.

Margaret Chan

Some countries that I go to are still trying to deny that it's happening. In India, 2.1 million people are living with HIV AIDS. India manufactures most of the drugs that are used to cure HIV around the world, which is an amazing, amazing fact that most people don't know.

Sharon Stone

Small aids to individuals, large aid to masses.

Maria Mitchell

I learned to speak first, and then to sign. I have never really known what it was like to hear, so I can't compare hearing aids to normal hearing.

Marlee Matlin

Rumors of sneezing, kissing, tears, sweat, and saliva spreading AIDS caused people to panic.

Ryan White

My own child, one of them, died of AIDS. A brilliant boy.

Kenneth Kaunda

AIDS and malaria and TB are national security issues. A worldwide program to get a start on dealing with these issues would cost about $25 billion... It's, what, a few months in Iraq.

Jared Diamond

I fight AIDS because it's a killer disease, destroys the human race in all fields.

Kenneth Kaunda

AIDS today is not a death sentence. It can be treated as a chronic illness, or a chronic disease.

Yusuf Hamied

An AIDS-free generation would mean that virtually no child is born with HIV; that, as those children grow up, their risk of becoming infected is far lower than it is today; and that those who become infected can access treatment to help prevent them from developing AIDS and from passing the virus on to others.

Anthony Fauci

Housing Works is the coolest thrift store in the world, because not only are they the best thrift store - they're not the most thrifty thrift store - but they have amazing stuff and all of their proceeds go directly to kids, mostly homeless kids, living with AIDS and HIV in New York, in the metropolitan area.

Ezra Miller

Americans think African writers will write about the exotic, about wildlife, poverty, maybe AIDS. They come to Africa and African books with certain expectations.

Chimamanda Ngozi Adichie

We started the AIDS virus. We are only able to maintain our level of living by making sure that Third World people live in grinding poverty.

Jeremiah Wright

I go to this gym full of stunt men. There aren't any TVs or treadmills there. This is a spit-and-sawdust kind of place. It has a lot of great training aids - trampolines and bags and every weapon ever invented to do harm to a human being. If you want to know how to throw a knife, it's great.

Jason Statham

The president recognizes that funding global health is good for national security, domestic health and global diplomacy. Consequently, President Obama has steadily increased funding for the President's Emergency Plan for AIDS Relief, or PEPFAR, which was created by President Bush and has strong bipartisan support.

Ezekiel Emanuel

AIDS is a horrible disease, and the people who catch it deserve compassion.

Sam Kinison

To me, AIDS is an international epidemic and every country can be affected by it. Therefore, it can be discussed on an international level. Unfortunately, AIDS doesn't require a visa.

Abbas Kiarostami

I had a dream, in 1985, I believe, when a friend I'd gone to school with was sick - one of the first people I knew who'd gotten the AIDS virus. I had a dream of him in his bedroom with an angel crashing through the ceiling. I wrote a poem called 'Angels in America.' I've never looked at the poem since the day I wrote it.

Tony Kushner

Living with AIDS is like always having the sword of Damocles over your head. The disease is scarier than death itself. The disease is so messy, so devastating, so pervasive. It robs you of everything you hold dear.

Larry Kramer

I have always made a distinction between healing and curing. To me, 'healed' represents a condition of one's life; 'cured' relates strictly to one's physical condition. In other words, there may be healed quadriplegics and AIDS patients, and cured cancer patients who are leading unhealthy lives.

Bernie Siegel

Even though it is the case that poverty is linked to AIDS, in the sense that Africa is poor and they have a lot of AIDS, it's not necessarily the case that improving poverty - at least in the short run, that improving exports and improving development - it's not necessarily the case that that's going to lead to a decline in HIV prevalence.

Emily Oster

Being, belief and reason are pure relations, which cannot be dealt with absolutely, and are not things but pure scholastic concepts, signs for understanding, not for worshipping, aids to awaken our attention, not to fetter it.

Johann Georg Hamann

Reiterating the belief that HIV is the cause of AIDS is an easy thing to do. Understanding the science and politics of the situation is much more complicated and requires study with a critical and open mind.

Nate Mendel

There's a huge AIDS epidemic in Africa, and one of Bad Boy's plans this year is to give more awareness to that. We're gonna be doing a big charity concert helping to save some of the brothers and sisters in Africa.

Sean Combs

The U.S. government has in recent years fought what it termed wars against AIDs, drug abuse, poverty, illiteracy and terrorism. Each of those wars has budgets, legislation, offices, officials, letterhead - everything necessary in a bureaucracy to tell you something is real.

Bruce Jackson

New drugs and surgical techniques offer promise in the fight against cancer, Alzheimer's, tuberculosis, AIDS, and a host of other life-threatening diseases. Animal research has been, and continues to be, fundamental to advancements in medicine.

Daniel Akaka

You can't be involved in healthcare without being involved in the battle against AIDS.

Paul Wolfowitz

I have covered wars, before the epidemic began and since. They are all ugly and painful and unjust, but for me, nothing has matched the dread I felt while walking through the Castro, the Village, or Dupont Circle at the height of the AIDS epidemic.

Michael Specter

The film itself involves a New York City radio storyteller, Gabriel Noone, who strikes up a friendship with one of his fans, an abused 14-year-old teenager who is suffering from AIDS, who does not have much longer to live.

Armistead Maupin

I had a calling inside of me. I had a sense that when I was going through experiences like living on the streets, losing my parents to AIDS, just having my whole world turned upside-down, there was this feeling inside of me like I was meant for something greater.

Liz Murray

C. Everett 'Chic' Koop became U.S. Surgeon General under President Reagan. He was a world renowned pediatric surgeon who had a tumultuous Senate confirmation process due to partisanship. Chic took office in January 1982, a time of 'tobacco wars' and a new and evolving terrifying disease that we ultimately came to know as AIDS.

Richard Carmona

I've worked with a lot of gay and lesbian organizations. I sit on the board of the Empire State Pride Agenda. I've also done a lot of work for Broadway Care/Equity Fights AIDS. I think it's important because, when we can be of service to others, it only enhances our lives. I've been helped a lot in my life.

Billy Porter

Sometimes Christians live in a terror of universal obligation: AIDS over here, people to be saved over here, a crushing sense of low-level guilt every day of our lives. Question to ask: Where has God put me right now? I need to say no to a whole bunch of other things because if I don't say no I can't say yes to others.

Kevin DeYoung

Pandemics do not occur randomly. From malaria and influenza to AIDS and SARS, the lethal microbes have come, in the first instance, from animals, especially wild animals. And we increasingly know which parts of the world pose the greatest risk for future incursions.

Nathan Wolfe

To me, celebrity doesn't mean a whole lot unless you're willing to use it. So I wanted to use it in a different way, with my AIDS work, the human rights stuff for the gay and lesbian community and the speaking I do.

Judith Light

I can cure AIDS, and I will.

Yahya Jammeh

It's funny... you can make fun of AIDS or Haiti, but if you make fun of some starlet in Hollywood's looks? That's like the one thing... the line you are not to cross.

Daniel Tosh

I sometimes wish I had been educated a Catholic, in order to unite the poetry of religion with its higher principles. Are they necessarily inseparable? Is man really so much of a philosopher, that he can conceive of truth in its abstract purity, and divest life and the affections of all the aids of the imagination?

James Fenimore Cooper

I came from Yale, where you get an extracurricular degree in self-importance because you went there. When AIDS happened, I was treated like an outcast. And I don't like that feeling.

Larry Kramer

We didn't exist. Ronald Reagan didn't say the word 'AIDS' until 1987. I've tried desperately to get a meeting in the White House; Gay Men's Health Crisis is already an established organization. I have a certain presence.

Larry Kramer

The stories my pupils told me were astonishing. One told how he had witnessed his cousin being shot in the back five times; another how his parents had died of AIDS. Another said that he'd probably been to more funerals than parties in his young life. For me - someone who had had an idyllic, happy childhood - this was staggering.

Erin Gruwell

Those who say that climate change doesn't exist are being understood as the flat-earthers that they are, as the people who deny the link between smoking and cancer, as the people who denied the link between HIV and AIDS.

Nicholas Stern

I went to Africa without the perspective of a balance between teaching people the truth, which has been my calling, and helping people who have physical problems, like AIDS and orphans and hunger.

Bruce Wilkinson

I don't think I could compare myself to Macaulay Culkin, because we're pretty much two different kinds of actors. He's done a lot of comedy. He does mostly just comedy like 'Uncle Buck' and 'Home Alone' and 'Home Alone 2.' And I've done a lot of different stuff, like sad movies, like the movie about the kid with AIDS.

Brian Bonsall

I've always wanted to write a book relating my experiences growing up as a deaf child in Chicago. Contrary to what people might think, it wasn't all about hearing aids and speech classes or frustrations.

Marlee Matlin

You should know that I've been hearing-impaired, not quite since birth, but I've been wearing hearing aids since I was 13, so I'm very conscious of the difficulty of voice communication.

Vint Cerf

Wouldn't it be great if you could only get AIDS by giving money to television preachers?

Elayne Boosler

I remember the '80s being about the Cold War and Reagan and the homeless problem and AIDS. To me, it was kind of a dark, depressing time.

John Cusack

To date, nearly 100,000 Hispanics have died with AIDS. Since Hispanics are the fastest growing minority group in the United States, our challenge is even greater.

Solomon Ortiz

On December 17, 1984, I had surgery to remove two inches of my left lung due to pneumonia. After two hours of surgery the doctors told my mother I had AIDS.

Ryan White

I take it to heart that, for example, there aren't enough funds for AIDS research, but people pay 20 times the value of an item of clothing.

Azzedine Alaia

The music aids the message, it's there to punctuate and abbreviate and shape the silence.

Saul Williams

AIDS is a plague - numerically, statistically and by any definition known to modern public health - though no one in authority has the guts to call it one.

Larry Kramer

I tell people that if I'm ignoring them, chances are I may not have heard them. I depend on hearing aids, but I've not found it a problem. I'm visually very aware!

Joseph Mawle

The AIDS is a disease that is hard to talk about.

Bill Gates

The fight against AIDS in China is already well underway. The Chinese government and other funders are providing major support, and they'll continue to bear primary responsibility for delivering prevention and treatment.

Bill Gates

Any charity that aids or supports trying to find a cure for cancer is very close to my heart. My mom had cancer multiple times, so it's something that I can relate to.

Jennette McCurdy

I burned out on AIDS and did no AIDS work for a couple of years. I was so angry that people were still getting this disease that nobody can give you - you have to go out and get it!

Harvey Fierstein

People with AIDS, cancer and other illnesses need free nonmedical support services.

Marianne Williamson

An educated child earns more later in life, knows how to keep their own children from dying, produces more food, is less likely to get AIDS, and in the case of boys, is less likely to engage in armed civil conflict.

Marianne Williamson

The radical right is so homophobic that they're blaming global warming on the AIDS quilt.

Dennis Miller

I think these last 10 years have seen just a huge shift in the psyche of this country as regards gay people. I think AIDS had a lot to do with it. So many families who really believed they'd 'never met one' were suddenly confronted with their sons becoming ill, and friends of sons. I think that brought a lot of it into the open.

Janis Ian

If African countries can unite and pull resources together, then that will be the best thing we could ever do for the problems in Africa including AIDS.

Ziggy Marley

The greatest grand challenge for any scientist is discovering how to prevent the spread of HIV and finding the cure or an effective vaccine for AIDS.

Philip Emeagwali

I go to Malawi twice a year. It's where two of my children were adopted from, and I have a lot of projects there that I go and check up on and children who I look after. It's sort of a commitment that I've made to this country and the hundreds of thousands of children there who have been orphaned by AIDS.

Madonna Ciccone

It doesn't upset artists to find out that artists used lenses or mirrors or other aids, but it certainly does upset the art historians.

Chuck Close

The heart of the security agenda is protecting lives - and we now know that the number of people who will die of AIDS in the first decade of the 21st Century will rival the number that died in all the wars in all the decades of the 20th century.

Al Gore

I have had lots of friends who've been affected by Aids and a very good friend of mine, Oscar Moore, died of Aids and I was with him in his last year quite a bit. And of course he was a

man living in a very rich culture with a wealthy family who
was able to afford health care.

Emma Thompson

The trouble is it's very difficult to pin-point the most important
thing because Aids affects everyone in different levels of
society, differently and you have to respond to it differently.

Emma Thompson

In Africa through the 1990s, with notable exceptions in
Senegal and Uganda, nearly all the ruling powers denied they
had a problem with AIDS.

Barton Gellman

I felt like calling attention to AIDS. I had the AIDS ribbon
colored into my hair during the playoffs in '95.

Dennis Rodman

In acting, there's a type of courage you're recognized for all the
time. You lose 100 pounds and play a guy with AIDS, and you
get rewarded. But, in life, doing what is courageous is quiet,
and no one knows about it. Courage is someone making
sacrifices for their family or making selfless decisions for what
they hope or feel.

Rob Lowe

This AIDS stuff is pretty scary. I hope I don't get it.

Robert Mapplethorpe

Anything that has a relationship with pleasure, we reject it. Eating, they talk about cholesterol; making love, they talk about AIDS; you talk about smoking, they talk about cancer. It's a very sick society that rejects pleasure.

Marjane Satrapi

We must have safe places where people can discuss and be treated. Forty-four million people are already dead from AIDS. What logic is there in not discussing the word?

Sharon Stone

AIDS is an absolutely tragic disease. The argument about AIDS' being some kind of divine retribution is crap.

Calvin Klein

If I were offered a cochlear implant today, I would prefer not to have one. But that's not a statement about hearing aids or cochlear implants. It's about who you are.

Marlee Matlin

The hearing aids are very helpful for speech reading. Without the hearing aids, my voice becomes very loud, and I cannot control the quality of my voice.

Marlee Matlin

Pneumonia is a disease that often flies under the radar of not just the public but even the global health community. It kills more children under 5 years old every year than AIDS, malaria, and measles combined.

Mandy Moore

The school I was going to said they had no guidelines for a person with AIDS.

Ryan White

One thing I can take credit for, along with the rest of show business, is when the red ribbons were out, we cured AIDS. Any advancements that came towards fighting AIDS were not done by scientists or doctors - it was people with little ribbons on their lapels.

Gilbert Gottfried

Epidemics historically have tended to kill the very young and the very old, but AIDS is different: Those ages 20 to 40 are most affected, which means that so far over 12 million African children have been orphaned because of AIDS.

Marvin Olasky

Most recently my battle has been against AIDS and the discrimination surrounding it.

Ryan White

If we stop exploring space, we're going to lose the same part of us that found vaccines and penicillin, the part that searches for cures to cancer and AIDS.

Corbin Bernsen

All of my peers died of AIDS, and I have no one to celebrate my past or my journey, or to help me pass down stories to the next generation. We lost an entire generation of storytellers with HIV.

David Mixner

I'm in awe of the AIDS workers in Africa who teach there, year in and year out.

Jordana Spiro

The African Union has to act in order to put an end to armed conflicts that undermine the continent, to fight against the devastation caused by AIDS and other contagious diseases, to promote sustainable development of its member states.

Omar Bongo

We must encourage people to get educated, to get tested, to get involved in the fight against AIDS.

Gwen Moore

In the earliest years of the AIDS crisis, there were many gay men who were unable to come out about the fact that their lovers were ill, A, and then dead, B. They were unable to get access to the hospital to see their lover, unable to call their parents and say, 'I have just lost the love of my life.'

Judith Butler

AIDS win be our first priority, but in two years' time we don't know where AIDS research will stand, so we are also thinking of activity on other diseases.

Luc Montagnier

I'm part of a team that raises millions of dollars and raises awareness of HIV and AIDS all over the world.

Linda Evangelista

I have a file of letters and bits of ephemera from friends who have died. I have had lots of friends who died of AIDS.

Rachel Maddow

AIDS is the biggest challenge, the major disaster facing this country and we would have wished for something more specific and far-reaching.

Mangosuthu Buthelezi

Think about it: Look at the strides of awareness and treatment and tests that women have had with breast cancer, that the gay community has had with AIDS, because they're active and they talk about it.

Herbie Mann

And so popular culture raises issues that are very important, actually, in the country I think. You get issues of the First Amendment rights and issues of drug use, issues of AIDS, and things like that all arise naturally out of pop culture.

Kurt Loder

AIDS was allowed to happen. It is a plague that need not have happened. It is a plague that could have been contained from the very beginning.

Larry Kramer

It's not really that I've been an advocate for hearing aids for a long time, it's just that I've been losing my hearing for a long time! So it's actually very important for me because I'm actually hearing impaired and I simply want to hear better!

Leslie Nielsen

Being in the design industry, I've tended to meet more people who are affected by HIV and AIDS.

Douglas Wilson

How is AIDS research to progress when the premise of science is questioning but the premise of questioning HIV is considered so dangerous that even venturing into the facts is too great a risk?

Nate Mendel

In the '70s, the gay movement was really making strides. Huge strides. And then AIDS came along and slapped a judgment on it all and the Right Wing religious movement was like, 'See. This is why, we told you.' And it pushed back the movement 30 years.

Mario Cantone

In fact, a large majority of those have died and of those expected to die of AIDS, as well as of those who are infected with the virus, are in sub-Saharan Africa.

Claudio Hummes

The Internet is emblematic of an era in which what happens in Southeast Asia or southern Africa - from democratic advances to deforestation to the fight against aids - can affect Americans. As has been observed about water pollution, we all live downstream now.

Shashi Tharoor

I'd worked for, during one period, for a PR firm, and for a while Rock Hudson was a client of ours, so I knew him well, and I knew when he had AIDS, that he had AIDS, but I would not write about that.

Robert Osborne

I lost a very dear friend who lived with AIDS for about 17 years. Rejecting early treatments that were iffy, he thought he saved himself. I really miss him a lot.

Bernadette Peters

Reducing the price of AIDS drugs gave me so much satisfaction that I've been thinking what else I could do. One day, I thought, 'Let's look at cancer and see how we can spare cancer patients' unnecessary suffering.'

Yusuf Hamied

I think Ed Koch is the person most responsible for allowing AIDS to get out of control. It happened here first, on his watch. If he had done what any moral human being should have done in the beginning, and put out alarms, then a lot fewer people would have gotten sick.

Larry Kramer

There's no question that the gay movement would not be as far along as it is without AIDS. But how can there be any other issue in the face of death, possible extinction?

Larry Kramer

Too many people hate the people that AIDS most affects: gay people and people of color. I do not mean dislike, or feel uncomfortable with. I mean hate. Downright hate. Down and dirty hate.

Larry Kramer

That the AIDS pandemic is threatening sustainable development in Africa only reinforces the reality that health is at the center of sustainable development.

Gro Harlem Brundtland

AIDS does not inevitably lead to death, especially if you suppress the co-factors that support the disease. It is very important to tell this to people who are infected.

Luc Montagnier

The challenges surrounding HIV and AIDS are getting more complex and mature, and we just can't stick our heads in the sand and say 'it can't happen to me.'

Brande Roderick

You will never catch up with the spread of AIDS no matter how much money, no matter how many antiretrovirals are put into the system, unless you stop its growth. And the only way to stop its growth is prevention.

Richard Holbrooke

When the AIDS epidemic broke, because I happened to be a science nerd and knew a lot about viruses and a lot about that virus at the time, I felt a moral obligation to go out and try to stem the fear and get out and explain to people what the disease was and how it worked.

Morgan Fairchild

As for AIDS, it's a plague. We are human, we get plagues. They come along every so often, kill off two thirds of the population; in the next generation it's a quarter; after that it's a childhood disease.

Larry Niven

It is my mission to ensure that HIV-positive children and children with AIDS are no longer overlooked and that they begin receiving the treatment and care they deserve.

Mike DeWine

Hospital-acquired infections are now killing more people every year in the United States than die from AIDS or cancer or car accidents combined - about 100,000.

Janine Benyus

AIDS is a judgment we have brought upon ourselves.

Mary Whitehouse

The virus that causes AIDS is the trickiest pathogen scientists have ever confronted. It mutates furiously, it has decoys to evade the immune system, it attacks the very cells that are trying to fight it, and it quickly hides itself in your genome.

Seth Berkley

When AIDS first appeared, people didn't know what it was. You'll remember that it affected mostly young gay men - it was actually called GRID for a short period of time: Gay-Related Immunodeficiency Syndrome - and people thought it actually might be recreational drugs or other types of toxins.

Seth Berkley

Perhaps more than any other disease before or since, syphilis in early modern Europe provoked the kind of widespread moral panic that AIDS revived when it struck America in the 1980s.

Peter Lewis Allen

I have great trouble with the people who envision AIDS as a punishment from God.

Russell Johnson

The message has become clearer to the nation about AIDS. People used to think they could catch it all kinds of ways, but we now know that it is absolutely passed through bodily fluids.

Loretta Devine

My play Safe Sex was picked apart because critics thought it was untrue. It was a play in which no one had AIDS, but the characters talked about how it was going to change their lives.

Harvey Fierstein

AIDS occupies such a large part in our awareness because of what it has been taken to represent. It seems the very model of all the catastrophes privileged populations feel await them.

Susan Sontag

We have common enemies today. It's called childhood poverty. It's called cancer. It's called AIDS. It's called Parkinson's. It's called Muscular Dystrophy.

Jerry Doyle

The media in America is not covering American AIDS very much. They're covering African AIDS as if somehow miraculously it's all stopped here. Well, it hasn't, and the one thing they're not saying about Africa is that all those people are going to die; there's no way these people can be saved - none.

Larry Kramer

We're still leaderless. We still don't have strong organizations that are fighting for us; there isn't a national AIDS organization out there worth squat in my opinion.

Larry Kramer

George W. Bush is very popular in Sub-Saharan Africa. Why? Because of PEPFAR, the President's Emergency Program for AIDS Relief.

Hillary Clinton

Do freshman philosophy classes nowadays debate updated versions of the age-old questions? Like, how could a merciful God allow AIDS, childhood cancers, tsunamis and Dick Cheney?

Dick Cavett

India has an enormous amount of AIDS awareness.

Sharon Stone

Africa the continent is not just what we see on the news. It's... not AIDS, and it's not just war and poverty. It's so much more. It's an abundant continent, and Botswana is an abundant place.

Jill Scott

Early in 1986, the World Health Organization in Geneva still regarded AIDS as an ailment of the promiscuous few.

Barton Gellman

In 1995, Glaxo bought Burroughs Wellcome and became the presumptive leader in AIDS therapy.

Barton Gellman

When you ask people what they think of Africa, they think of AIDS, genocide, disasters, famine.

Mo Ibrahim

As a nation we should commit ourselves not only to the fight against terrorism, but to economic justice, defeat of the AIDS epidemic and vestiges of discriminatory policies of all kinds.

Charles B. Rangel

Drug manufacturers could afford to sell AIDS drugs in Africa at virtually any discount. The companies said they did not do so because Africa lacked the requisite infrastructure.

Barton Gellman

For a decade, makers of AIDS medicines had rejected the idea of lowering prices in poor countries for fear of eroding profits in rich ones. The position required a balancing act, because the companies had to deflect attacks on the global reach of their patents, which granted exclusive marketing rights for antiretroviral drugs.

Barton Gellman

In the wealthy industrialized nations, effective drug therapies against AIDS became available - AZT as early as 1987, then combinations of antiretroviral agents in 1996. The new drugs offered hope that fatal complications might be staved off and AIDS rendered a chronic condition.

Barton Gellman

The first and pivotal negotiations over global access to AIDS drugs began in Geneva in 1991. They lasted two years, but confidential minutes suggest they were doomed the first day.

Barton Gellman

The first reports of AIDS closely followed the inauguration of President Ronald Reagan, whose 'family values' agenda and alliance with Christian conservatives associated AIDS with deviance and sin.

Barton Gellman

Throughout the early and mid-1990s, the Clinton administration debated the merits of paying for AIDS testing and counseling of vulnerable populations overseas.

Barton Gellman

AIDS had won gays sympathy; they no longer seemed the privileged brats that the general populace had resented in the 1970s.

Edmund White

I asked my body if it was going to die or not from AIDS. And it said 'no.' I sort of paid attention to that.

Edmund White

When my lover Hubert Sorin was dying of AIDS, he was always trying to fix me up - posthumously, as it were - with the cute busboy at the hotel.

Edmund White

I've had the privilege of working with Bono for the past few years in the One Campaign to fight AIDS and hunger and disease around the world. Bono is an Irishman and a great humanitarian. And I remember him telling me of his admiration for America.

Mike Huckabee

I can remember in the late 1980s and early 1990s how many men with AIDS I saw everywhere in Key West. There were hospices and medical supply stores geared to people with AIDS. It seemed that every sick man who could afford it had headed for the warmth and the tranquillity and the gay-friendliness of the island.

Edmund White

In Paris, AIDS was dismissed as an American phobia until French people started dying; then everyone said, 'Well, you have to die some way or another.' If Americans were hysterical and pragmatic, the French were fatalistic: depressed but determined to keep the party going.

Edmund White

African-American women account for 67 percent of all newly diagnosed female AIDS cases.

Elijah Cummings

I run a modest-sized laboratory that's looking specifically at what we call 'the pathogenic mechanisms of HIV disease, or AIDS.'

Anthony Fauci

If a country denies it has AIDS, that country will inevitably become an even greater victim.

Richard Holbrooke

Because I am not formally trained in the medical sciences, I can bring in new ideas to AIDS research and the cross-fertilization of ideas from different fields could be a valuable contribution to finding the cure for AIDS.

Philip Emeagwali

I started to write about science and medicine at the 'Washington Post,' in the early days of the AIDS epidemic.

Michael Specter

I think AIDS can be won. I think we can win this fight. It is winnable. But it means behavior change.

Franklin Graham

The desire to move into a bigger house, to avoid living AIDS daily, and a dream to be accepted by a community and school, became possible and a reality with a movie about my life, The Ryan White Story.

Ryan White

My mom's brother was gay, and he actually passed away from AIDS when I was 13. He was quite a character, but he also worked at the electrical plant, so he was this complicated guy with a big laugh who would wear a trucker hat and do impressions. He was gay, but to me, Uncle Alan was just the funniest person in the world.

Casey Wilson

The discovery of HIV in 1983 and the proof that it was the cause of AIDS in 1984 were the first major scientific breakthroughs that provided a specific target for blood-screening tests and opened the doorway to the development of antiretroviral medications.

Anthony Fauci

I have serious hearing loss. I'm challenged if I don't have my hearing aids in.

Al Jarreau

United Nations peacekeepers are going all over the world spreading AIDS even while they're trying to bring peace. What a supreme irony.

Richard Holbrooke

I think we all realize that anyone can - and has - gotten AIDS. So there's obviously still a lot to be done.

Eric McCormack

I came to N.Y.C. in 1988 and got very involved with Act Up. I also started making movies, including two very gay shorts,

'Vaudeville' and 'Lady.' It was the height of the AIDS epidemic, and New York City was both dying and very alive at the same time.

Ira Sachs

From 1989 to 2000, I was focusing in on my children. I hadn't realized the world had changed a lot. AIDS had happened, for starters, and so many people in the arts died or were affected.

Daphne Guinness

There are two things that I put my focus on. One is the fight against AIDS and finding a cure. The other is human rights.

Judith Light

We were taking collections for people with AIDS in New York around Easter.

Chita Rivera

I remember my first friend who got sick. It was 1981, and the disease was called the gay cancer. I don't think the word 'AIDS' came out until '84. I just remember it being terrifying as more people got sick. We didn't know how you could catch it, you heard all kinds of crazy things.

Ellen Barkin

When there's a terrible illness like AIDS sweeping through, you help people.

Bernadette Peters

I'm doing a very funny show in which we talk about issues. I speak at Aids charities and things. It's great to do something fun with our days and yet we're told we're doing something important.

Eric McCormack

It's wonderful that so many people want to contribute to fighting aids or malaria. But, if somebody isn't paying attention to the overall health system in the country, a whole lot of money can be wasted.

Paul Wolfowitz

The film was made in 1973. It was a golden time for people to experiment without risking, for example, AIDS. Today one has to be so much more careful and I don't think a character like that could exist now.

Sylvia Kristel

It was quite a ride and very conflicting for me, too - to be nominated for an Oscar, to be straight and healthy, and to be getting all these accolades while these people around me were suffering and dying from AIDS.

Bruce Davison

The male elites that run most countries are exceedingly uncomfortable with the subject of AIDS because it's a sexually transmitted disease.

Richard Holbrooke

www.ingramcontent.com/pod-product-compliance
Lightning Source LLC
Chambersburg PA
CBHW072017290526
45787CB00013B/1237